RAISED BED GARDENING

An Easy Guide to Growing Organic Vegetables with Your Thriving Raised Bed Garden Month by Month

HANNAH ROSES

 *Copyright @ 2020 Hannah Roses - All rights reserved*

This book is written with the sole purpose of providing relevant information on a specific topic for which every reasonable effort has been made to ensure that it is both accurate and reasonable. Nevertheless, by purchasing this eBook you consent to the fact that the author, as well as the publisher, are in no way experts on the topics contained herein, regardless of any claims as such that may be made within. As such, any suggestions or recommendations that are made within are done so purely for entertainment value. It is recommended that you always consult a professional, prior to undertaking any of the advice or techniques discussed within.

This is a legally binding declaration that is considered both valid and fair by both the Committee of Publishers Association and the American Bar Association and should be considered as legally binding within the United States.

The reproduction, transmission, and duplication of any of the content found herein, including any specific or extended information will be done as an illegal act regardless of the end form the information ultimately takes. This includes copied versions of the work both physical, digital and audio unless express consent of the Publisher is provided beforehand. Any additional rights reserved.

Furthermore, the information that can be found within the pages described forthwith shall be considered both accurate and truthful when it comes to the recounting of facts. As such, any use, correct or incorrect, of the provided information will render the Publisher free of responsibility as to the actions taken outside of their direct purview. Regardless, there are zero scenarios where the original author or the Publisher can be deemed liable in any fashion for any damages or hardships that may result from any of the information discussed herein.

Additionally, the information in the following pages is intended only for informational purposes and should thus be thought of as universal. As befitting its nature, it is presented without assurance regarding its prolonged validity or interim quality. Trademarks that are mentioned are done without written consent and can in no way be considered an endorsement from the trademark holder.

Credit cover image: by congerdesign – Pixabay.com

Table of Contents

INTRODUCTION 7
CHAPTER ONE - Vegetal Garden Planning 11
    How to Plan a Vegetable Garden 13
CHAPTER TWO - Building a Raised Bed Gardening 17
    How to Build a Raised Bed Gardening Step by Step 20
    Maintain a Raised Bed 22
    Advantages of Raised Bed Gardening 24
CHAPTER THREE - Types of Water Irrigation System 27
    1. Hand Sprayers Irrigation 30
    2. Sprinklers 30
    3. Drip Irrigation Systems. 31
    4. Greenhouse Irrigation 32
    5. Running water system 33
CHAPTER FOUR - How to Make the Right Compost 35
    How to make compost 40
CHAPTER FIVE - The Right Vegetables Month by Month 47
CHAPTER SIX - Growing Herbs 53
    Herbs For You To Grow in Your Garden 60
    Basil 60
    Dill 61
    Lavender 62
CHAPTER SEVEN - Growing fruit 63
    1) Appletree 64
    2) Peartree 67

- 3) Quince Apple 70
- 4) Cherry 71
- 5) Amarasco 72
- 6) Peach 73
- 7) Apricot 74
- 8) Lemon 75

CHAPTER EIGHT - Growing Vegetables 77
- Why is it important to grow your own vegetables? 79
- Vegetables to grow in your home garden 83
  - 1) Tomatoes (Lycopersicon esculentum) 83
  - 2) Radishes (Raphanus sativus) 84
  - 3) Zucchini (Cucurbita pepo) 85
  - 4) Beetroot (Beta vulgaris) 85
  - 5) Carrots (Daucus carota) 86
  - 6) Spinach (Spinacia oleracea) 87
  - 7) Peas (Pisum sativum) 87
  - 8) Peppers (Capsicum annuum) 88
  - 9) Lettuce (Lactuca Sativa) 89
  - 10) Onion (Allium cepa) 89

CHAPTER NINE - Types of Fertilizer for your garden 91

CHAPTER TEN - Pests, prevention and treatment 97
- Aphids 97
- Larvae or caterpillars 98
- Whitefly 99
- Leaf miners 100
- Chapulines 100
- Red spider 101

- Trips 101
- Mealybugs 102
- Snails and slugs 102
- Nematodes 103
- Vegetable Gardening Problems – Prevention 103
- Treat a garden against pests 105
- CONCLUSION 109

INTRODUCTION

Growing plants in raised beds have many great benefits. One of the greatest benefits is the ability to produce more from the same area. Elevated bed gardens can actually double or triple the amount of space harvested produce! This is because the square footage required for pathways is considerably reduced, and more space can be dedicated to plants.

Another great advantage of growing in elevated beds is that you can change the soil quality more readily, and you can also grow plants in highly inhospitable soil. If your garden is typically very sandy, or you have lots of clay, growing in it can be difficult. But if you have a raised bed, you can simply put in the frame your own purchased or created soil mix and grow your plants.

Weeds are often much less a concern in the traditional elevated bed. Since the soil is limited, any weeds that pop up are easier to find, and the weed seeds in the current soil are buried under just too much soil to sprout in most cases.

Gardening is no longer limited to yard-houses. Today, one can build an indoor beautiful, and serene garden. Many people now use raised beds for indoor gardening. These beds are good for flowers and vegetables. Additionally, the height of the beds decreases the back pressure you get when dealing with traditional garden beds with constant bending.

The design of higher garden beds is an excellent way for new gardeners to first green their fingers. Easier to manage than traditional beds, lifted beds can take you from the safety of the garden, or garden path – without worrying about pushing your flowerbed soil underfoot. This is able to compress the soil around the roots of your plants, raising their air contact to grow.

A combination of soil and compost can be used on a raised garden bed, eliminating from the garden the risk of 'poor dirt,' an issue that faces multiple gardeners in urban areas. With raised bed gardening, Water Drainage is more effective, making the plants easier to respire once again.

Raised Garden Beds are garden beds that are raised above the surrounding soil or ground on which they are constructed, and are typically supported by some kind of frame. These frames can be made of different materials, blocks, bricks, stones, or wood. A hung garden bed can also be seen as an uplifting bed.

With the comfort that the garden does not normally exceed 4 feet in, and for any duration, the height of the raised bed is set. The 4-foot-dimension is because one can touch from both sides the middle of the garden. A downside with a bed that's long is that when performing a specific task that involves the entire bed width, such as planting or weeding, it makes for a long walk around the Gardens Bed. 4 feet by 8 feet high garden bed is usually considered to be a suitable size for most gardeners, both for gardening and for 8 feet, which is a standard wooden size that can be purchased at most lumberyards.

One major advantage is that the amount of edge available is increased by dividing a long garden bed into a shorter portion. There is a definition of permaculture that needs to be identified or to understand the "edge effect" and the interaction between two media, the intersection of which meet different environments. This interaction between two different ecosystems provides a broader range of favorable environmental conditions that improve both the life of the animals and plants.

Raised beds also have the ability to plant crops closer together because they don't have to spacewalking paths, and so the traditional walking method is more productive per square foot. The benefits of higher-density planting are also that plants grow together, shade exposed soil, and suppress weed growth.

A raised bed garden would also benefit from the opportunity to maintain a better soil condition. Due to the easy access of an elevated gardens' bed, no compaction is found in the soil that is normally caused by walking in the conventional row gardening method. If the soil is maintained changed with organic matter, the natural life of the soil will function for you. The structure of the soil in a raised garden bed will profit greatly and will bring back productive cultivation.

CHAPTER ONE
Vegetal Garden Planning

Starting a new project is always a good idea, with a simple plan in mind. Map out a plan for the vegetable garden based on the desired result you like. Consider your family size, and then work on the premise that it takes about 100 square meters to feed a family of four during the year. First, consider the climatic conditions in which you live; you can not grow vegetables all year round if it is cold. The garden that you design will need to be bigger in this case so you can grow extra vegetables.

The climate is generally divided into dry, temperate and tropical when planning a vegetable garden. You will need to do some research on the type of climate conditions prevailing in your part of the world and the vegetables that thrive in this environment. That is the perfect way to design a vegetable garden. You will move on to the next part of the plan once you have a plan and know what vegetables to produce and how to layout the garden.

Identify and order a good store for your seeds long before planting time, so you're ready to grow when it starts. With organic gardening techniques, you can opt to germinate the seeds separately and then plant them as seedlings. When you have large plantings on your list, schedule the germination of the seeds, so you don't end up maturing all of them at the same time.

Now you have to concentrate on the program, growing vegetables to grow in your garden. Each plant has different needs, and you will have to consider that when planning your vegetable garden. In colder climates, plants that can survive frost include cauliflower, turnips, brussels sprouts, broccoli, snow peas and onions.

A mild disposition is essential for vegetables, including carrots, parsnips, leek, salads, celery and cod. If you try to develop them out of season, you might end up with nothing for your table. The warm seasonal vegetables like potatoes, tomatoes, eggplants, beans, corn and capsicums do not live and die. Most of their growth will be in warm weather months.

You will do your own research and decide exactly what to develop and when. Don't let nurseries talk about buying seeds that won't yield anything because planting them is the wrong time of year. Find the following gardening tips while preparing your garden.

- The cool winds stun your plant growth, and the hot winds dry out the soil and damage the plants, and the plants are destroyed by extra-strong winds. To protect the plants, you may have to prepare a windbreak.
- It takes at least five hours of sunshine every day when you find your yard, so you have direct sunlight.
- Taller plants should not be positioned where smaller plants obstruct the sunlight. Before you start planting, monitoring the sun's path through your garden may not be a bad idea.
- Structure up your compost stack and proceed to top it, it is the easiest way to naturally fertilize your garden. Plant rotation is nice as it does not give the pests much chance to invade the crop.

How to Plan a Vegetable Garden

Many of us, just a sketch, would have drawn our gardens to decide the room we have and help us choose the plants we would grow. To ensure the time you spend preparing your garden is as successful as possible, there are a few main questions to ask yourself.

A well-designed garden with a raised bed

Many of us will have drawn our gardens, even a sketch, to determine the space we have and to help us choose the plants we will grow. There are a few key questions to ask yourself to ensure that the time you spend planning your garden is as productive as possible.

How many plants can I grow in the space I have?

One of the most common mistakes of gardeners is to try to pile up too many crops in their gardens, which leads to overcrowding and poor harvests as the plants grow and compete for the best nutrients.

What is the best layout for my plants?

It is usually necessary to rearrange the plants on a plan until you get the perfect arrangement. For example, sprawling squash should be at the edge of vegetable beds so as not to suffocate other crops, leafy crops like summer lettuce can benefit from the shade provided by taller plants, and sweet corn should always be grown in blocks rather than in a single row so that they can reproduce correctly by the wind.

What do I need to buy or order?

It is essential to carefully plan orders for seeds and garden supplies so that you can start growing as soon as the weather permits.

When should I plant?

It is important to establish a calendar of the best times to plant each crop in your area. For best results, some crops such as tomatoes and peppers should be started under cover or indoors several weeks before your last frost. Other crops such as beans and squash cannot be sown until the outside temperatures are warm enough.

What could go wrong?

Think about what could be causing the problems. For example, large blocks of crops can easily be attacked by pests like aphids, so be sure to include flowering plants to attract beneficial insects to your plan, or a sudden heatwave could paralyze young people. Tender plants unless you have provided adequate irrigation or adequate shade.

All of this planning can be done with a pen and paper, but it can be time-consuming. It gets more and more complicated as more plants are grown, especially if you take into account several years of crop rotation plans.

CHAPTER TWO
Building a Raised Bed Gardening

The advantages of growing on raised beds are many; first of all, with this technique, it will be much easier to differentiate the soil according to the needs of the plant, compared to the classic cultivation on the ground.

By opting for this type of cultivation it will also be much more convenient and quick to work the soil and carry out all maintenance operations, it will be possible to drastically reduce the problem of weeds and, by avoiding compacting the soil with foot traffic, it will also allow a better flow of air and water to the roots of the plants.

Another important advantage is that by deciding to grow our vegetables, rather than aromatic herbs or flowering plants, using the raised bed technique, it will also be possible to do it on the balcony, on the terrace or perhaps in an area of the garden that was previously unused because it has no land with the right characteristics.

In essence, this cultivation technique consists of raising the land destined for the plants and delimiting the different crops through the creation of simple structures obtained by assembling wooden planks rather than bricks or stones of various kinds.

Gardening raised beds is a practice that was used long before colonial times. It has become increasingly popular among home gardeners because they can be installed in small inconvenient places of entry, it is a solution for gardening on land that can be installed almost anywhere in a limited period of time. They are also a perfect way to attach an appealing aspect to your yard and can bring other advantages as well as being a workplace than a dug garden.

The elevated beds are garden beds that are designed higher than the surrounding land. They are constructed no wider than four feet so that work in them is easy to reach. The length you want them to be can be any length. The distance is kept small, and there's no need to walk on the field to avoid compacting the soil.

The advantages of a raised bedside garden include easy access to the farm, better management of soil conditions and higher yields with less square footage. They are a good choice for construction in areas of poor soil like poor drainage or rocky areas.

This gardening method is much less difficult for disease and pest control. The soil structure will greatly benefit from the mulching and the accompanying planting and create a healthier plant that can defend itself against these problems. The addition of organic mulch will also improve the structure of the soil and feed the microorganisms living in the soil. These microorganisms are necessary to work the soil and add nutrients necessary for plants to thrive.

Raised garden beds are a wonderful idea. Depending on the size of the gardens, you can complete most of the weekends, create and plant a raised bed garden to blend in with your yards' natural environment and attract wildlife, including birds and butterflies.

A safe and environmentally friendly way of gardening. Organic gardening is in harmony with nature, away from gardening. A healthy and productive crop is produced so that both you and the environment are healthier.

How to Build a Raised Bed Gardening Step by Step

The 'contained lifted garden bed' is the most commonly lifted bed. For several vegetable and herbal gardens as well as flower gardens, it provides perfect growing conditions. Many fruits also do well in raised garden beds, including strawberries, grapes and raspberries.

Steps for a wooden upholstered bed as most elevated beds are made from wood.

Step One

Selecting a location is one of the most important decisions you make while building an elevated bed garden. Select a region that gets full sun, as most vegetables need full sun. If you want to plant vegetables that require partial sunlight, either build another bed in a different location or find a location that receives complete and partial sunlight. Also, make sure the area is flat, so water is easy, and all areas receive constant and equal amounts of water. If you want to make watering quick, consider installing a quick-to-use drip irrigation system to keep your garden watered.

Step Two

Decide your garden size and shape. Make sure you can reach all of your gardens without going into bed. Try to keep the garden long and narrow, allowing you to access all your vegetables without actually entering the garden. That's nice because the soil won't get compressed from running over it. This will give you carrots growing as straight as an arrow. Note accessibility is important, and if you want to place your garden against a fence, try to make it just 3 feet long so you don't have to walk into the garden. The depth of an elevated bed garden is up to you, but the deeper, the better, especially if you grow carrots or parsnips that need deeper soil. If you can, make your bed 12 inches tall!

Step Three

Your site's planning is very critical. Once you have your garden shape and scale, start building the bed. Grab the existing sod and loosen the soil below to a depth of eight to twelve inches. This gives your garden extra depth and good drainage. To move quickly, just cover the current sod and soil with newspaper or cardboard.

Step Four

Now it's time to build the bed. Using rot-resistant lumber like cedar or one of the newer composite woods to create your bed. Depending on the size of the garden, 'two by six' pieces of wood will create the entire garden. Cut the pieces to the appropriate length, add them to a simple frame. There are several different ways to add the wood, but choose one that is simple for you and can hold well for years of use.

Step Five

After building the frame in a spot, make sure you level your bed from all directions. This is a necessary move because if your bed is not level, you will find that water flows off one section of the garden and sits in another. If part of your frame is high, just remove any under it until you have a level frame.

Step Six

It's time to fill your garden with soil and compost after leveling. This will allow you to create a garden with great soil, ideal for growing vegetables. You can plant or sow seeds when they are full and raked.

Maintain a Raised Bed

The raised bed gives plants better protection against frost and pests than a flower bed because of its height. However, to avoid invasion or frost damage, some maintenance needs to be done.

The best way to manage aphids and cryptogamic diseases is by preventive steps. By properly combining plants, chemical plant protection products can be avoided. Certain varieties of flowers and vegetables release substances that are beneficial to other species through their leaves and roots. Chervil, then, is scaring snails and aphids. Plant species also each have specific requirements for nutrients. They are made more resistant by the combined crops and fertilizers.

You should create a protective fence around the edge of your flowerbed, to prevent snails from attacking your salads. A fine mesh screen, placed on the ground, protects your crops against voles. Special coatings reduce the risk of cryptogamic diseases, root and trunk rot, as well. The wooden beds have to be lined with a pool cover, as a precaution.

If you grow perennials or grow under a frame, you'll need a protective film, a winter veil, or a blanket to protect your bed from frost in winter. You can also shelter your plants there if you have a greenhouse.

Wash the soil layer from time to time using a rake and take advantage of this to remove weeds, to increase the quality of water and nutrients. Biodegradation causes the soil to sag over time, making it necessary to add a small amount of soil. Even if you regularly fertilize your flowerbed, after six years, you'll need to replace all the layers of soil. The humus layers are indeed exhausted after this time, and the draining layer no longer fulfills its role.

Advantages of Raised Bed Gardening

Gardening is no longer restricted to yard-houses. Today, one can build an indoor beautiful and serene garden. Many people now use raised beds for indoor gardening. These beds are good for flowers and vegetables. Additionally, the height of the beds decreases the back pressure you get when dealing with traditional garden beds with constant bending.

There are many advantages to gardening with raised beds. Most of them are here:

- Not only are raised beds easy to maintain, but they are also less prone to certain types of weeds. So, it avoids the unnecessary use of herbicides. Other than that, when the soil quality isn't very good, raised beds are ideal. Raised beds to allow you to control the soil quality, so you can plant different plant types using different soil qualities.
- The excess humidity is not retained when you plant flowers or vegetables. So the roots get a chance to breathe freely. This is especially useful when heavy showers are provided in the field, which tends to erode the soil. In this case, the water is fast draining away, and the soil is not eroding. So, you're not going to face a waterlogging crisis or ruined soil.

- Another benefit of this bed style is optimizing the available space. You can grow plants close to each other without overcrowding, which increases yields.
- As the soil is above the ground, it's going to warm up faster than a conventional flower bed. This warmth will help to improve and improve plant growth.
- Rising beds are ideal for seniors who want to indulge in gardening without putting undue strain on their backs. People with back problems are also benefited.

CHAPTER THREE
Types of Water Irrigation System

Garden needs water to grow well. Many people prefer a garden irrigation system to water it themselves. Most people think of only one option, which is the massive irrigation network used in large fields. These sprinklers are usually expensive and hard to install. They can also be complicated. The good news, however, is that smaller irrigation systems are available for personal gardens. They are user-friendly, energy- and water-efficient.

As you know, rainwater is planting water's best source. Modern irrigation system uses plant rainwater. It also minimizes your water and energy bill. Rainwater irrigation systems come with a timer, and you can program it as you like. These systems styles can be modified based on garden needs. Considering the garden layout, the sprinklers are mounted on that basis.

The sprinklers will be placed in the garden at regular intervals, using existing pipes. Installation requires linking pipework and adding water jets. It's so easy you can do it yourself. If you build yourself, it will dramatically reduce the cost.

Thousands of homeowners spend millions on water-irrigation systems each year. Watering your lawn by hand is neither fun nor effective. Plants and gardens need watering regularly. If you wait until it's time to rescue your plant from near-death then expect it to recover immediately, the plant will be put too much stress on. Too little water followed by too much water is an invitation to disease and other issues and is very bad for the plant's overall health.

The solution is being consistent, and the way forward is to establish a routine. Only shaking a hose and making the leaves wet doesn't put any water on the roots and is completely pointless, so you'll have to water the plant again the next day because the roots are dry. The number one best solution to this is to buy a long water wand attachment so that you can channel a large volume of water directly to the roots or where you want it to go at low pressure.

A general rule of thumb that differs because of the country where you live is that the average lawn requires about one inch of water a week. Place a few small rain gauges around your yard to make sure you're thorough and reliable. By using these gauges, you will know how effective your irrigation is and whether things need to be adjusted so that certain areas get less and others get more. Irrigating takes a lot of guesswork.

Deciding where the plants are located in an extremely critical and productive way of maintaining water in irrigation. Random planting is rather slow and adds even more work when you manually spray. You should have a plan for the laying out of your lawn before you begin the landscape. The best thing you can do is to create beds of similar plants, which will make maintenance and watering much easier.

Early in the morning, most experts found that watering your lawn or the garden was the most effective way. When you do so during the day's immediate heat, as much as 50%-60% may evaporate before it enters the dirt and is effective for the roots. The biggest tip I can't emphasize enough, if you are using an automatic water supply timer, is that you don't need to water the pelvis. A large deal of water can also be conserved.

Home irrigation is often done by a simple hose attached to the outside faucet of the home, but this is not the most cost-effective system for the owner as well as plant health. Instead, homeowners have many different options to use this ineffective method to water plants to water their lawn, garden or flowers. These systems can be used either on their own or in combination, depending on the landscape layout and the type of plants that need watering.

1. Hand Sprayers Irrigation

The most common ones are probably sprayers that attach to tubing and are used directly by hand in water plants. These are the most inefficient products for water plants and require the most effort. The cheapest and easiest to set up are, however. Aware consumers should also reduce the water expended on enhancing their inconveniences.

2. Sprinklers

For water lawns and plants, sprinklers may be used. They are available in a wide variety of styles and sizes so that they can be both the type of plants that are used and a specific landscape. These minimize the effort needed for water areas, although they still have the problem of spreading large amounts of water not used by crops. It is best used in large areas of grass.

Advantages of sprinkler irrigation

- It suits almost all types of soil;
- It can be adapted for different types of topography;
- It can be mobile or fixed;
- Uniform application in the plantation;
- It can be used together with fertigation;
- Low risk of soil erosion.

Disadvantages of sprinkler irrigation

- High implementation cost;
- Low efficiency in places with strong winds;
- Low effectiveness in places with high temperatures;
- Need for a clean source and free of water residues.

3. Drip Irrigation Systems.

These products use tube lengths in the garden on the next floor. When activated, they directly give the plant roots drops of water. These products are the most efficient watering method for plants and cost the least in water.

Often known as drop-by-drop irrigation. This type of irrigation is used in areas where water is scarce and significantly optimizes this resource. The operation idea is to distribute the water through drippers, which will moisturize the root zone of each plant.

There are several benefits to this irrigation system: it holds water well, it is well controlled, the water directly reaches every plant or crop, its installation is easy. It is simply a general tube diversified into small PVC pipes, with small mouths supplying water to each particular plant or crop.

You can also add timers or automatic systems, which will make the job much easier. It is a commonly used device as it mostly prevents the growth of mold or vegetation, apart from holding the moisture very well. It may cause the nozzles that water each plant to spoil after a long period of time, or because of bad weather conditions, but this is not a very common issue.

4. Greenhouse Irrigation

A combination of sprinklers and drip irrigation systems can completely water a whole greenhouse for greenhouse owners as well as increase the level of humidity within a greenhouse to improve plant health. These systems are fitted with hoses and feature miniature sprinklers that directly spray into specific pots.

Greenhouse irrigation systems are made up of different elements, which vary according to the needs and particularities of irrigation for each crop or farmer.

In greenhouses are plants that are not irrigated from the water that comes from the atmosphere, but must be watered by the implementation of an irrigation system if we want them to be well cultivated, which conserve humidity and they grow.

First, it is important to analyze the conditions that these plants need and to decide which irrigation system is the one that will guarantee better results. These types of irrigation regulate air humidity and soil temperature.

Greenhouse watering systems come in many shapes, shapes and sizes. One of the first things you need to remember when developing greenhouse watering systems is the demand you would need in terms of the type of garden you water. Mind also that some plants may require more water and some less. With certain watering systems, you will be able to automate the watering needed for each plant, so one of the first things you need to do is to measure your needs. This phase is possibly the most critical in an automatic irrigation system of the sort.

5. Running water system

It is the irrigation system that can best adapt to the needs of each farmer or the person who is going to install it. But this irrigation is the most common technique of collecting water from the middle barrels and PVC pipes.

One of the greatest advantages you see in this irrigation is that you save a lot of costs and it's a total ecological system as well.

CHAPTER FOUR
How to Make the Right Compost

Compost is a high-quality organic fertilizer. It improves the structure of the soil, increases the amount of organic matter and provides nutrients, especially micronutrients such as nitrogen, potassium and phosphorus. It contains all the nutrients necessary for the healthy growth of plants and releases them slowly, which allows a continuous contribution. Its correct application favors the improvement of gardening conditions and can perfectly substitute manure.

The compost is formed by the decomposition of organic products; This serves to fertilize the land. Organic matter decomposes aerobically (with oxygen). This can be formed by different types of organic waste, such as the remains of fruits, vegetables, animal feces, leaves, eggshells and tea bags.

Compost is the result of the fermentation of organic or vegetable waste. To optimize the fermentation, it is essential to have a high humidity level and good ventilation of the compost.

Place your composter in a shaded place, and above all, do not make a "floor" or concrete screed below the composter. It is very important that the compost is in direct contact with the soil of your garden. Larvae, insects, earthworms, fungi, and bacteria will "nest" in the compost. They promote the ventilation of your compost, degrade waste, and improve the quality of your compost.

The compost is what remains after you have started a process of composting household. That is the process of decomposition and humification on residues of organic substances, such as the leaves of your garden, the grass cut from the lawn, etc.

Depending on the composting method that you have adopted, you will get a different type of compost, but basically, they can be categorized into three types:

- fresh compost
- ready compost

- ripe compost

The fresh compost (from 2 to 4 months in the case of composting with the heap) is still being transformed. Being still rich in nutrients, it is excellent as a fertilizer and for plant growth. Be careful, however, to apply it directly to the roots because this compost is still not very stable.

The compost ready (from 5 to 8 months), however, is stable, since the decomposition process does not produce more heat. On the other hand, it is less suitable for use as a fertilizer. We recommend using it in vegetable gardens or gardens as fertilizer before sowing or transplanting.

The mature compost (12/18 or 24 months) is the most stable one. Therefore, it is the least suitable as a fertilizer. However, it is perfect in direct contact with the roots or seeds and as potting soil for potted plants or even in the case of re-seeding and mowing of lawns.

Importance and benefits of compost

At some point, everyone can start working on the land or building gardens inside our homes. If we started planting the bean seeds as children in kindergarten, or already out of necessity.

But something that is highly needed to help nutritiously and healthily grow what we sow is compost. Also known as organic fertilizer that helps the plants grow well.

It is a scientific fact that organic matter is an extremely significant soil fertility element. This helps to considerably enhance the earth's stability and properties, both physical and chemical.

Compost is an element by itself which can be formed naturally with the materials provided by the earth. If they are very much of animal or vegetable matter, they return to earth at the end of their life cycle.

We may help generate it in the same way that it is created naturally by recycling the waste in our homes. This will help boost the plants' health and growth, so they will get better nutrients for them.

The use of compost helps to improve soil efficiency by reducing abrupt temperature changes. Additionally, fertilizer use is also very detrimental to soil and compost substitutes for soil-affecting chemicals.

Importance and benefits of compost

The garbage that is collected in our homes commonly has as final destination the dumps of the cities. Places that are sources of infection and that can cause a lot of damage to the skin, eyes and respiratory tract.

It is very important to create awareness in our communities regarding the contamination produced by garbage. That is why we share five beneficial aspects of composting in our homes and parks.

- It returns nutrients to the soil, controls erosion and prevents soil wear caused by rain washing.
- It corrects the structure of the soils and acts as a sponge that retains water, which gradually releases to the benefit of the plants.
- It retains moisture and allows air to pass through.
- Recycle and reduce the volume of organic waste, to convert it into compost.
- It serves as an antibiotic against microorganisms.

If we reduce the production of waste in our home, we could positively impact the total balance of pollution. Therefore, we all have the task of making our own habitat a safe and clean place.

How to make compost

Making compost, or composting doesn't just mean building and keeping a compost bin in order. It also means knowing and controlling what you're pouring into it to get a good fertilizer. This book will give you simple guidelines on what you should be doing and what you should not be putting into compost. Follow the three "Rs" (Reduce, Reuse and Recycle) to reduce the amount of waste that needs to be thrown away!

We said that by compost, we mean the product of the decomposition, accelerated and controlled by man, of organic substances. Among these, kitchen scraps. Mainly vegetable remains fruit peels, coffee and tea grounds, eggshells, fireplace ash, etc.

But also gardening. For example, pruning branches, mowing of lawns, dry leaves, withered flowers, garden waste.

The advantages of compost

Home composting offers several advantages.

First of all, it guarantees the correct closure of the waste cycle, given that the workforce makes up about a third of the total amount of household waste. The compost DIY avoids landfill or to ' incinerator, thereby reducing disposal costs. At the end of the home composting procedure, then we will have a natural organic fertilizer available.

This will be usable in the vegetable garden, in the garden, or for potted plants instead of chemical fertilizer pollutants. We will thus save money by limiting the purchase of potting soil, substrates, and organic fertilizers. And at the same time, we will reduce the atmospheric pollution produced by the combustion of these waste, also avoiding the infiltration of leachate into the soil.

The compost, such as natural organic fertilizer, gradually releases into the soil the elements indispensable for the development of the plant, such as nitrogen, phosphorus, potassium, and trace elements.

What can become compost and what cannot

Anyone wishing to proceed to home composting must first of all pay attention to what to put in the composter.

The kitchen and gardening wastes indicated above, as well as other biodegradable materials, are doing well. These include uncoated paper, cardboard, sawdust, and shavings from untreated wood.

Attention, all glass, plastic, and metal objects, synthetic fabrics, chemicals, expired drugs, coated paper, and litters of dogs and cats must be absolutely avoided.

With great caution, leftovers of food of animal origin and foods cooked in small quantities can also be added. Same warning for leaves of plants resistant to degradation (magnolia, beech, chestnut, conifer needles, etc.).

How to make compost: cumulative composting

We now come to the various forms of composting. The most widespread is certainly the cumulative one. Here we will have to choose places that are practicable all year round, irritable, and located in the shade of trees that lose their leaves in winter. In winter, we must allow solar radiation, while in summer, the sunlight must be mitigated. Placing chopped wood under the pile (10-15 cm) is another good practice to avoid mud formation in the winter months.

The minimum height of the pile must be 50-60 cm in order to retain heat and guarantee microbial activity. However, the 1.3-1.5 meters must not be exceeded. Otherwise, the material risks compacting under its weight.

The best form in the summer is the trapeze shape. It allows you to adequately absorb rain and replace evaporated water. In winter, on the contrary, it is good practice to use the triangular one, to avoid the excessive accumulation of rain inside the pile, given the poorer evaporation.

The secrets to making a good compost

The secret to successful composting is in the correct mixing of the waste. This activity is essential to allow the right activity of microorganisms and avoid the onset of putrefaction phenomena, with the consequent bad smells.

In practice, it is necessary to create a correct stratification, alternating the most humid and nitrogen waste (grass clippings and kitchen residues), with the drier and more carbonaceous ones (shredded branches, broken cardboard, wood chips, dry leaves, straw, etc.).), which guarantee good porosity and the correct supply of oxygen to the pile. The initial water content must be between 45 and 65%, while as regards the right nitrogen-carbon ratio, it is good to know that for each gram of the first one, you need 20 or 30 of the second.

To ensure the correct supply of humidity, the pile can be covered during rainy periods with materials such as "non-woven" or jute sheets or layers of leaves and straw of 5-10 cm. In this way, we will be able to retain water without compromising air circulation. The cover can also be useful to protect from excessive drying during the summer months.

Another aspect that should not be underestimated for the success of composting is the right oxygenation. It is essential for bacteria that perform aerobic biodegradation. For a correct exchange of air, it is, therefore, necessary not to compress the material of the pile and turn it periodically with a pitchfork, an operation to be repeated frequently if the cluster is not very porous.

How to make compost: the fertilizer

An alternative to cumulation can be the manure. It consists of a hole dug in the ground where to accumulate organic waste. In this case, however, problems may arise due to the tendency to accumulate too much water, especially in the case of the waterproofed substrate.

Another typical problem is the insufficient exchange of oxygen with the outside by the materials deposited on the bottom.

Those who choose this system will, therefore, have to take some precautions. Among these, the insertion of drainage pipes, a layer of gravel, or a pallet under the organic material placed in the hole.

The same pallets can also be used to separate the waste from the hole wall, in order to guarantee a good exchange of air.

How to make compost using the composter

As can be guessed, the heap is particularly suitable for those who live in houses with large gardens that produce large quantities of twigs and green waste. The composter made of plastic, wood or network instead is more useful for those citizens who are gardens of small and medium-size, originating less waste.

They are containers of variable volumes (from 200 to 1,000 liters), with various types of openings. Their use allows limiting the visual impact of decomposing materials, ensuring their sanitation and less affected by atmospheric conditions. However, there may be difficulties in turning the material over if they cannot be opened on one side. If you intend to purchase a plastic composter, prefer those that have systems that promote air circulation in the internal walls.

But how does a composter work?

The operation of these tools is very simple. After having sorted, simply insert a layer of coarse twigs at its base, then alternately adding layers of nitrogen and carbonaceous waste, according to the same principle analyzed previously. After 3-4 months, the vegetable waste must be turned over and then put back into the composter.

After 5-6 months, the lower part of the waste, brown in color and similar to the humus of the undergrowth, will have produced a homogeneous compost that is already available for use. This fraction must, therefore, be sieved and left to dry in the sun for a few days. The wood waste not yet transformed must instead be reintroduced into the composter.

Of course, the use of these do-it-yourself tools implies the same adoption of good practices as for cumulation. First of all, it is necessary to ensure proper mixing by alternating nitrogen and carbon layers. Then it is necessary to ensure good air circulation by inserting coarse twigs and turning the material once every six months. Finally, it is necessary to maintain optimal humidity (55-60%), which favors the reproduction of aerobic microorganisms.

Generally, compost is ready after about 12-20 weeks in winter and 10-15 in summer. The completion of its degradation is evident both from the appearance and form the characteristic smell.

CHAPTER FIVE
The Right Vegetables Month by Month

Growing your own vegetables is a very fun pastime, which also has many beneficial benefits such as healthy food (you know what additives were used if any), exercise, outdoor work etc. Growing your own vegetables is also a wonderful activity for the entire family to participate, as it helps kids understand better how nature works and where food comes from.

Some people think a lot of space is needed to grow your own vegetables. When you are trying to provide the family with a range of vegetables every day of the year, this is definitely real. It's not true if you cultivate your own vegetables to complement your grocery shopping to have some fresh vegetables. For example, four or so runner bean (Pole Bean) plants in a patio container should provide more than enough beans for a family of four for a few months.

When it comes to vegetables, each country in the world has different varieties that grow best in their specific climate, even in some countries a specific crop that grows well in one region does not grow at all in another as the climate and atmosphere are different. It's here where some of the fun comes into growing your own because you can experiment with different vegetable varieties from different parts of the world to see what you can and can't produce, experimentation will also be required to establish specific growing conditions for these unique varieties for your environment.

There are two ways to have our own gardens at home, in the external area (backyard) or in the internal area (kitchen, balcony, balcony, service area). Let's deal with the first way, which will probably be subject to the weather. The success of a vegetable garden, in this case, is directly related to the right moment of each planting of herbs, vegetables, and vegetables. Each month has its characteristics, which make them more suitable for each species.

The plants are different from each other in relation to the type of soil and temperatures necessary for their full development, so it is very important to know what are the most suitable options for each season of the year.

Below, we have prepared a list of the most used plants in vegetable gardens and which month, or months, are most suitable for planting.

- **January:** lettuce, watercress, celery, various cabbages, radish, almond, turnip, beet, arugula, chicory, spinach, sweet potato, parsley, coriander, purslane, carrot, Brussels sprouts, and cabbage;

- **February:** watercress, lettuce, chicory, beans, parsley, radish, cabbage, beets, cabbage, peas, spinach, and beans;
- **March:** carrot, almond, parsley, garlic, lettuce, chicory, spinach, celery, miscellaneous cabbages, cauliflower, broccoli, cabbage, watercress, celery, onion, coriander, peas, beans, beans, strawberry, turnip, radish, and cabbage ;
- **April:** watercress, almond, beet, turnip, parsley, garlic, arugula, chicory, celery, cauliflower, broccoli, cabbage, spinach, carrot, coriander, pea, asparagus, broad bean, lentil, strawberry, radish, lettuce, onion, and various cabbages;
- **May:** radish, carrot, almond, turnip, beet, arugula, parsley, chicory, celery, spinach, cauliflower, broccoli, winter cabbage, garlic, lettuce, potato, onion, various cabbages, fava, and strawberry;
- **June:** almond, carrot, turnip, beet, arugula, garlic, chicory, watercress, cauliflower, broccoli and winter cabbage;
- **July:** pea, almond, arugula, garlic, lettuce, radish, chicory, beet, broad bean, and cabbage;
- **August:** artichoke, white celery, jiló, eggplant, various peppers, peppers, tomatoes, onion, cabbage, asparagus, strawberry, melon, watermelon, and cucumber;

- **September:** lettuce, radish, beet, carrot, miscellaneous cabbages, cauliflower, broccoli, jiló, eggplant, miscellaneous peppers, peppers, tomatoes, squash, zucchini, green beans, cucumber, gherkin, parsley, coriander, onion, peas, spinach, fava beans, lentils, melons, watermelons, and turnips;
- **October:** chard, carrot, various cabbages, cauliflower, broccoli, cabbage, various peppers, peppers, tomatoes, eggplant, jiló, pumpkin, zucchini, green beans, cucumber, gherkin, mandioquinha, parsley, potato, sweet potato, coriander, watercress, lettuce, beet, broccoli, chicory, cumin, broad bean, melon, watermelon, turnip, radish, thyme, onion, and tomato;
- **November:** pumpkin, watercress, lettuce, radish, carrot, broccoli, cabbage, various cabbages, cauliflower, sweet potato, coriander, beet, spinach, beans, melon, watermelon, turnip, cucumber, and various peppers;
- **December:** pumpkin, zucchini, green beans, cucumber, carrots, cabbage, watercress, lettuce, beets, broccoli, various cabbages, spinach, melon, watermelon, turnip, various peppers, and radish.

There are still many herbs that are considered perennial, produce all year round, such as sage, parsley, chives, marjoram, basil, for example, but that cannot resist very low temperatures or frosts, so it is interesting that they are planted in more protected places.

Another important point to note is the use of greenhouses; for example, some plants in greenhouses have their productivity extended for many more months.

The other option, mentioned above, of growing a vegetable garden indoors is ideal for those who live in apartments and dream of having an organic garden without pesticides. This can be done in pots and the location chosen for its location inside the house, allows you to decide less for the month of the year and more for the climate that we create in the indoor environment.

You can create light and temperature conditions for your favorite herbs. We have selected some garden options available for sale that can give you a good idea of how to build yours. They can stay in the kitchen, laundry area, on the balcony, in short, wherever there is space available for you to cultivate your new hobby.

CHAPTER SIX
Growing Herbs

The practice of growing herbs has been around for many thousands of years, and both medical and culinary uses for these herbs have taken place. Herbs give us fragrances and tastes in these modern days, and they are also a very important part of your kitchen garden.

The great thing about herbs is that you don't have a lot of lands to grow, and, really, a small plot will make several applications for you, and all your herbs for your personal use would be easy to grow.

Another endearing thing about growing herbs is that they are very easy to cultivate, and even people who have never grown anything before will have no problem raising herbs in their home gardens.

The best time to plant the herbs is during the spring months, and a wonderful herb garden can also be built in your home, which is attractive and helps to grow ample numbers of herbs. A formal herb garden includes the use of traditional growing techniques, many of which have originated from the ages. A knot garden, for example, lets you grow herbs that boast knotty designs, and this type of growth has been practiced since the Middle Ages.

You can also seed part of a flower garden or even a vegetable garden to plant the seeds when you do not have a lot of space for growing herbs. In particular, as this helps to create a wonderful curvature for each floral or vegetable garden, you might wish to grow creeping rosemary and thyme.

The difference between perennial and annual herbs is also significant. The former type can grow year after year and can be incorporated into your herb garden's basic structure. Annuals, on the other hand, must be cleared before the freeze begins to kill them and be snipped during the summer seasons.

Basil is an outstanding example of an annual herb and an essential part of many foods in the Mediterranean. It can easily be planted after its seeds are harvested, but you need to plant seedlings if you want to bloom in summer.

Why grow herbs?

Did you ever buy fresh herbs specifically for a recipe you're about to make at the grocery store? I did. This is an expensive buy, despite the number of herbs that are normally included. They also appear to degrade rapidly, unless careful care is taken to avoid damage.

Then why not go for dry herbs? Well, the fact is nothing beats the fresh kind of thing. Fresh herbs are more aromatic and have more flavor. Having an indoor or outdoor herb garden helps you to easily pick the herbs you need every day and make your home-made meals even more delicious.

Herbs can also have an ever-growing medicine cabinet or a ready-made supply of tea for you. They're also loved by pollinators, including bees and butterflies, which means the other plants will be healthier.

What do you need

To start with an herb garden, you need a few basics.

- Ground

Whether you plan indoors or outdoors, it doesn't matter, you'll need one, and you'll need a place to plant. That can be a number, a bed or containers raised up. You have an option, but be sure to check out the Common Errors section below for guidance on choosing your plants' best growing container.

Most herbs prefer conventional garden soil, but some Mediterranean plants need sandy soil well-drained. That includes the lavender, rosemary and berry. Check what your plants like, and group them together. For example, in a portion of your garden, you can add a small amount of sand to the garden soil for plants like dry plants. You may create a richer mix for those in another region who need more humidity.

Location, location, location

Most herbs love the sun, so pick a spot to get a generous amount of sun every day. Sunshine is important for healthy development, for at least 6 hours. However, the optimal location can vary, depending on the plant.

Some herbs like it dry, while others prefer a little bit of shade. For details that can help you pick the right location, you can check a seed packet, sticker, or mark on the pot (if you purchased your plant from a nursery)

You can mix tall plants that like to enjoy the sun with short plants that prefer some shade, with a little preparation. A giant parsley plant, for example, may provide shade for low-growing sweet grass.

A significant factor to remember when choosing a location is the distance between that location and your house. Can you face a rainstorm and get some chives for your early jamming? Would you care to stroll to the edge of your garden in search of a basil leaf while dinner is awaiting you?

Some people do not care a thing, but some may prefer to have their own herb garden nearby. Whatever you do, make sure it is easily available so you can keep a close eye on it and constantly harvest an endless supply of delicious spices and medicine.

Start your herb garden

It takes planning to create a good herb garden. Decide whether you want plants to grow in containers or in the field and whether you want to grow indoors, outdoors or both. You will also have to determine whether you want to continue using purchased seeds or plants.

Start the herbs inside

Do you have herb seeds to continue inside? You can choose to start planting and choose the "route from scratch," but for beginners, I don't recommend it. The rationale? Many seeds from herbs take a long time to germinate. Starting to grow annual plants and seeing them die in winter is also painful. Head into your nearest kindergarten to search for herbs available.

Plant herbs outside

When you've determined what you're planting, what kind of soil you need, and where to plant it, it's time to start. I like to make a diagram of my landscape, and then plan the grasses I want to put and where taking the height and width of the plants into account.

Instead, it depends on the herbs. In your current soil blend, garden dirt, sand, and/or moss. It is then time to dig. Dig a hole twice the size of your plant's root ball, remove the plant from the pot and loosen the roots. Place the plant in the pit and soil backfill.

Donate plenty of water to the farm. I always think it helps to mark my plants with a clear label on stakes. Often the difference between young plants is difficult to say, so a label makes all the difference.

If they are perennial, the herbs should be planted in the spring, but during the growing season, you can plant annuals almost anytime. I like planting annuals like cilantro regularly every few weeks, so my supply is constant throughout the year.

Container gardening

You may also grow the herbs outdoors or indoors in containers. If you need to, it's a perfect way to make sure you can push your plants around, and it can help prevent weeds like mint.

When selecting the container process, be sure to use a container that is wide and deep enough for your mature grass and has plenty of holes at the bottom to allow water to drain out. Put plenty of rocks or pottery pieces in the bottom, so drainage is possible.

For arid herbs, fill the container with compost or sand compost. Plant your grass, and soak it.

Caring for your herb garden

The rules are straight forward. Herbs mimic any other herb. They need to grow on light, water, and nutrients. When it comes to herbs, there's no special trick. Harvest by gathering or cutting the leaves, as required. Watch for weeds and look out for possible pests before they get into your garden so you can easily get rid of them in the event of an attack.

While herbs in your garden are no harder to grow than tomato plants in your vegetable patch or roses, the problem is that many people prefer to plant different herbs together and treat them as one and the same thing. For this reason, it is so important to decide what your plants like before they are planted together in the soil.

This also refers to providing the plants with nutrients. Be sure to remember your plants prefer the amount of fertilizer and don't assume all herbs want the same amount.

Herbs For You To Grow in Your Garden

Basil - It is the most frequently cultivated herb and is well known to herbal garden enthusiasts worldwide. The herb Basil grows well in low humidity and moist soil climes. Spring is the ideal season to start growing the Basil plant, but only after all frost risks have been alleviated as this plant is extremely susceptible to cold temperatures and can be harmed if exposed.

It is important to note when planting Basil that each plant is approximately twelve inches apart. This allows the growing plant to access sufficient water and makes it a healthy plant.

After the planting of Basil, the development of mature leaves ready for harvest takes around six weeks. When the harvest is carried out, a proper drying method can lead to a savory dried plant, which can be used in a variety of recipes to delight your taste buds. In warm summer months, this robust herb would have grown to about one or two feet high and sprouting deep green or even pure leaves with tiny, white flowers.

Dill - Nothing could be easier than to cultivate the delicious Dill herb. Just a dispersion of grains thrown into your grassy garden will lead to stalks that can grow to four feet. The herbal set adds beauty and is used in many recipes. Dills Stalks have distinctive blue-green leaves, feathery and with striking yellow flowers.

The dill plant is a sun-loving plant that ensures a flourishing plant in areas with full exposure to sunlight. The best way to ensure a hardy crop is a gap of 8-10 inches between plants. You will go back about two weeks after sowing the seeds when the herbs exceed 1 inch in height and thin the area around each herb. This cycle ensures that each plant receives the necessary nutrient content from the soil and ensures that each plant is adequately exposed to sunlight.

Lavender - One of Lavender's most natural, fragrant herbs. This aromatic plant is a wonderful covering for any herb or flower garden because it grows delicate pink and purple flowers on high stalks. Lavender is a perennial plant, and in the middle of summer, it is at its best. Lavender is also an essential ingredient in aromatherapy, soap making and potpourri.

Although this hardy herb is easy to grow if choosing to start from seed form can require some extra work. The best way to implement this plant from your local gardening center is through fresh plants or root cuttings. These plants grow well in warm, alkaline-rich soil that is not water-logged. As the winter months close, the elegance of these plants will disappear, but in the next spring and summer seasons, these plants will return stronger and lusher than last.

CHAPTER SEVEN
Growing fruit

Growing fruit trees and fruiting shrubs is an operation that our vegetable greenhouse, greenhouse or balcony, whether small or huge, will never lack.

The juicy and tasty fruit is the perfect complement to the nutritious vegetables and aromatic herbs offered to us by our garden.

Also, if we're not thinking about a real orchard, two rows of strawberries and a currant plant in a small vegetable garden or greenhouse would suffice to give us some vitamin-rich dessert. The round bushes of wild strawberries may also be planted at the edges of a flowerbed, where they will act as a decorative frame for our vegetable garden or greenhouse as well as being an enticing treat to taste when walking.

On the other side, if we have more room available, we can grow a small fruit tree plantation, choosing the trees that best match the environment, height, sun exposure, and soil type in our garden.

The fruit trees, which remind us of the Garden of Eden's romantic pictures, cheer up our garden and balcony's green space and give us a beauty that is always different depending on the season but never banal. From the beautiful spring flowers to the lush and green foliage rich in summer fruits to the mystical autumn colors and the romantic and enigmatic winter forms.

So only a tiny fruit tree on the balcony will help us rediscover the sight and sense of wonder for the everyday wonders that we are sadly sometimes unable to see any more today. Having fruit trees in the garden or on the balcony is also a way to have always available seasonal fruits and vegetables, suitable for the preparation of fresh and nutritious extracts and juices.

Here is a selection of some fruit trees to be planted in the garden, in the vegetable garden or on the balcony, to be chosen according to our preferences, the climatic conditions of the place where we live and depending on the room we have available.

1) Appletree

The apple tree is part of the fruit of Pome, to which all the fruit trees belong, the pulp of which contains a core of small seed. The apple tree can be grown in a large or medium-sized garden as well as in small vegetable gardens, where spindle bushes are probably more suitable. There are several varieties of apple trees that adopt various stages of harvesting and maturing, and grow fruits with different flavors. The apples have many characteristics and are suggested for various sweet and savory recipes.

Growing tips

In humus-rich, very loamy soils, the apple tree grows especially well. Having a healthy humidity in the soil and a humid environment is very critical. Planting an apple tree on dry or southern slopes is not advisable, and while the apple tree is not an especially fragile fruit tree, it is best to select the right variety for the area we live in. The Golden Delicious variety grows well in mild climate areas, while Geheimrat Oldenburg and James Grieve will yield good harvests in harsh climate zones.

Also, the apple tree is a fruit tree that can never survive in isolation but needs a pollinating insect that fertilizes its seeds, including bees. Since most varieties are incompatible with each other, i.e., they can not pollinate themselves, and it is important to plant different varieties nearby. Excellent pollinating varieties and varieties are among the most popular crops that complement each other harmoniously, for example, Golden Delicious and Granny Smith. The apple tree is a plant that horizontally grows its roots, and most of the roots that accumulate nutrients are in the upper layer of the soil. For this reason, the area under the canopy, which will be periodically supplied with natural fertilizer and compost, is very important to take good care of.

Some of the most common and easy to grow varieties:

- **Clara:** slightly acid fruit with acid pulp. It contains about 15 mg of vitamin C on 100 grams of pulp. It should be harvested in July and eaten fresh.
- **Gravenstein:** tasty, sweet fruit with juicy pulp. It contains about 8 mg of vitamin C on 100 grams of pulp. It should be harvested from mid-August to mid-September and consumed until December.
- **James Grieve:** tasty fruit, sweet and with juicy pulp. It contains about 7 mg of vitamin C on 100 grams of pulp. It should be harvested from mid-September to mid-October and consumed up to the end of November.
- **Geheimrat Oldenburg:** fruit with an almost neutral flavor with juicy pulp. It contains about 1 mg of vitamin C on 100 grams of pulp. It should be harvested in September and consumed up to the end of December.
- **Goldparmane:** fruit with a sweet taste and crunchy pulp. It contains about 18 mg of vitamin C on 100 grams of pulp. It should be harvested from mid-September to mid-October and consumed from November to February.
- **Cox Orange:** fruit with a sweet and delicate flavor, with very juicy pulp. It contains up to 20 mg of vitamin C on 100 grams of pulp. It should be harvested in October and consumed until February.

- **Golden Delicious:** sweet and tasty fruit, the particular aroma of wine, tender and juicy pulp. It contains about 8 mg of vitamin C on 100 grams of pulp. It should be harvested from mid-October to mid-November and consumed from January to April.
- **Granny Smith:** fruit with green skin and a sour taste, with a crunchy and juicy pulp. It contains about 16 mg of vitamin C on 100 grams of pulp. It should be harvested in October and consumed until the end of February.

2) Peartree

The pear is a fruit tree belonging to the family of the Rosaceae and whose roots are not entirely understood, even though it is considered to be native to Asia. The spindle-shaped bush is particularly suitable for small family gardens, while you can choose medium or tall trees for medium-large gardens. The pear has rich properties and is ideal for many sweet and savory recipes. Pears are also commonly used in cooking for the preparation of centrifuges and extracts of fruits and vegetables.

Growing tips

The pear tree is a fruit tree that prefers the warm climate, has deep roots, and extends horizontally, so it needs deeper soil than the apple tree. The pear tree reacts to stagnant groundwater negatively and loves nutrient-rich, warm, rather light soils. Pear grows well, especially in a sunny position and needs the right partner for pollination, just like apple trees.

Some of the most common and easy to grow varieties:

- Angelica: fresh and aromatic fruit with a juicy pulp. The fruit is harvested from late August to early September and is harvested from the second half of September. This plant variety is particularly suitable for hill areas.
- Williams Christ: sweet and juicy fruit with very tender pulp. The fruit is harvested from mid-August to late September and ripens until the end of October. To be well

cultivated, this variety of plant needs a well-sheltered position.
- Good Luisa d'Avranches: sweet and juicy fruit, which is harvested in September and ripens until the end of October. This particular variety is suitable for cultivation only in warm areas.
- Favorita di Clapp: delicately acidic fruit with a juicy pulp, which is harvested from mid-August to mid-September and ripens until mid-October. This variety of plant is very vigorous and suitable for medium-altitude positions
- Beurrè Rocca: juicy and sugary fruit with a semi-fine pulp that is harvested from late August to mid-September and ripens until the end of October
- Conference: fruit with a sweet and delicate flavor and juicy and grainy pulp. The fruit is harvested from mid-September to mid-October and ripens until early December.
- Thigh: juicy and sugary fruit, which collects and ripens in July. This variety is suitable for very hot climates
- Spina Carpi: slightly acidic fruit with a juicy pulp that is harvested from late September to late October and ripens until late December. This variety is suitable for cool and windy hilly areas.

- Volpina: fruit with a slightly sour aroma and firm pulp, which is harvested in early October and ripens until the end of November. This variety is suitable for hill areas.

3) Quince Apple

The quince is a family Rosaceae plant, which develops in a tiny tree whose height does not exceed 4-5 meters. The quince is an ancient tree that has not undergone man-made modifications or grafts and is, in all probability, the tree that was present in Eden's garden. Quinces are poorly cultivated today, but quince plants are often inserted as rootstocks for pear and apple trees into orchards. Quinces have to be prepared to eat and are used in many national dishes' recipes. Quince is often grown as a shrub because it remains smaller in size, making growing and care easier.

Growing tips

The quince needed a lot of light and a not too heavy soil to grow. Unlike pears and apple trees, the quince is self-fertilizing, and only a single specimen can be found. Quince can also be grown in containers, and it spreads a good fragrance if held in the winter living room.

Some of the most common and easy to grow varieties:

- Champion: large and very fragrant fruits
- Meliform: large fruits and very abundant harvest
- Van Deman: fruit with excellent pulp flavor
- Kostantinopoler: a frost-resistant plant with large fruits

4) Cherry

The cherry belongs to the family of stone fruits, to which the fruit trees belong whose pulp contains a hard-shelled kernel that protects the seed. Both tall and fruit are the most common varieties of cherry only after 6-8 years. They are also not recommended for those who have a small vegetable garden or greenhouse, even because of the size of their leaves.

Growing tips

The cherry requires a dark, smooth, silky soil and not too moist to grow. It doesn't need special attention, if not the position: it must be put in full light. Since the cherry isn't self-fertilizing, at least two adjacent specimens must always be planted.

Some of the most common and easy to grow varieties:

- Durone di Vignola and Durone della Marca: hard-pulp fruits
- Precocchio della Marca e Goriziana: soft pulp fruits
- Bigarreau Napoleon and Bigarreau Moreau: semi-hard fruit

5) Amarasco

The Prunus Cerasus, commonly known as Amareno or Amarasco, is a Rosaceae family fruit tree whose fruit, black cherry, is one of the most delicious in our garden that we can find. There are also shrub-shaped with smaller dimensions, suitable for growing in the vegetable garden or in the greenhouse, but their fruits will be more acidic than larger trees. The best and easiest variety to grow is the Schattenmorelle, whose fruit is dark red in color and has a more acidic taste, while if you prefer a sweeter and juicier fruit, you will have to select the newer Morellenfeuer variety, which is well suited to all types of terrains.

Growing tips

Amarasco is a self-fertile species, so just plant one. These fruit trees grow well on all soils and become sick only when they are planted in hot, humid soil. We'll need to grow our fruit tree in a sunny position to have sweet and juicy black cherries. For a year, the amarasco fruit on the tree, which is why it is important to prune the branches periodically before a new jet is attacked to create an abundance of fruit annually.

6) Peach

The peach tree is a fruit tree that belongs to the family Rosaceae, originally from the Middle East. It is typically grown in its shrub-shaped form, ideal to be kept in the balcony, vegetable garden or flower pots. The most popular and easiest cultivable varieties are:

- Michelini: white, very aromatic, late flowering and less prone to frost
- Sant'Anna: scented pulp and excellent flavor
- Ceccarelli quince: yellow, aromatic and with an abundant harvest

Growing tips

The peach tree grows especially well in mild climate areas, as it requires a lot of heat and humus-rich soil. Avoid growing it in areas that are too cold and hot, unless it is in a specially protected area. Late frosts also threaten peach trees as they bloom in early spring (March-April). Peaches bear fruit for a year as well as amareno, and must, therefore, be pruned annually.

7) Apricot

The apricot is a fruit tree of uncertain origin, and some sources suggest that this tree would come from China, while others trace it back to Persia or Armenia. The apricot is a medium-sized plant, as it never goes beyond 5-7 meters in height, suitable for growing in your garden or in a small or medium-sized garden.

The most common and easiest varieties to grow are:

- Della Val Venosta: particularly suitable for cold areas, fragrant pulp and delicate flavor
- Nancy apricot: ancient French variety, abundant harvest with frost-sensitive flowers
- Reale d'Imola: sweet and fragrant pulp, easy to grow

Growing tips

In terms of climate, apricot trees are much more demanding than peaches: they generally grow well with mild temperatures and in a dry, clean, and nutrient-rich soil. These fruit trees are also vulnerable to the possibility of late frosts, such as peach trees. Many of the key dangers for this plant's proper growth is represented by strong winds, which, in particular, may cause very serious damage to bloom.

8) Lemon

Lemon is a fruit tree native to India and Indochina. This plant tolerates pot cultivation well because, in nature, it is a low-sized tree with vigorous but slow growth.

Growing tips

Lemon is a fruit tree that we can keep healthy in the garden or on the balcony, even in pots. However, to make it grow well, it is important to have a pot of the right size (the plant's foliage must be contained within the diameter of the pot), a porous, organic and draining soil (we suggest using material at the bottom of the pot which facilitates the water flow and prevents stagnation) and remember to repot at the beginning of the spring every two years. The lemon plant should be sheltered during the winter in warm and sunny surroundings with a minimum temperature of 13 degrees.

The most common and easy to grow varieties are:

- *Femminello comune*: the most common cultivar in Italy, it has medium vigor, and the fruit produces an abundant, clear and very aromatic juice.
- *Femminello syracusano*: this type of lemon is a plant of great vigor, with rapid growth and which bears fruit earlier than other Mediterranean lemons.
- *Femminello Apireno Continella*: compared to the common Femminello, it has the advantage of not having seeds but, on the other hand, has an excessively thick skin, the plant is thorny, and the fruits are small.
- *Monachello*: this is the Italian cultivar that absolutely resists badly dry, a fungal disease very common in fruit trees, especially citrus fruits.

CHAPTER EIGHT
Growing Vegetables

Some people enjoy growing vegetables in their garden, and if you're among those who want to grow vegetables in the garden, then using vegetable seeds and some useful techniques, you can easily grow your own vegetables in your backyard or greenhouse.

Many nursery shops hold Veg Seed varieties in their store; you can select the one that needs different efforts and grows in less time. Some of the Vegetable Seeds are cumin seeds, also referred to as jeera. It is warm and sharp in taste, and its scent persists for a long time in the food as it brings a different taste and flavors to the food. Cowpea-Kokand and sadabahar, these crop types can be grown during the season, and it takes about 45 to

50 days to germinate. It is medium height grass. Brinjal seeds are used to grow a high variety of brinjals and take 75 to 80 days to harvest.

Consider buying pesticides, insecticides and fertilizers after selecting vegetables. Pesticides and insecticides avoid soil and pest. Tomato feed is a strong soil fertilizer if you enjoy growing fruits like strawberries after harvesting. Tomato is a growing vegetable grown by most in their garden.

If you're new to agriculture, then it's suggested to help any experts or someone who has experience growing vegetables at home as experts can provide some valuable tips on growing vegetables, and they can also help you figure out your farming-related questions. Farming isn't that hard, as it seems, although it requires effort and time.

If you have less room or space at home or a small garden area, you can prefer growing vegetables in pots and containers. Most people live in apartments and multi-story houses, where they have no garden area. They can grow vegetables in containers and pots. It is also economical since less money is spent on food.

Any individual can grow the vegetables in their garden, though they need some expert advice. Just by growing vegetables in your home, you can provide a balanced diet for family and children. This helps kids adapt to eating healthy, nutritious food.

Why is it important to grow your own vegetables?

Whether it's a balcony, a terrace or a real field, almost always there's something for gardening! So why not combine pleasure with a little patch of vegetables? Compelling reasons for growing your own fruits and vegetables!

1 - Gardening is good for your health

A safe mind in a sound body! The exercise and the efforts it brings to gardening do you good. All the studies on the relationships between vegetation and living environment show the undeniable benefits of greenery's presence on our well-being! The daily gardening practice stimulates both the mental and the physical ... in short, taking care of the plants and your garden means taking care of yourself!

2 - Know what you are eating

It's our responsibility to eat well, and this responsibility is accentuated when we have kids we can only hope for the best. When we grow our own fruits and vegetables, we at least know what we eat! When you have children, it helps them realize that the source of food is not only the temples of consumption that are supermarkets but also in the vegetable field.

3 - Save money

Even with a small garden, it is several hundred euros less to spend in stores. Rodolphe Grosleziat claims to save the value of around three times the minimum wage by buying almost no fruit and vegetables anymore! To find out more, discover its anti-crisis vegetable patch.

4 - To have fun

Gardening is, above all, a pleasure. Touching the ground, watering or even flowering plants and growing fruit is incomparable. Gardening has a beneficial effect on mental health simply because it generates well-being linked to outdoor activity.

5- Cultivating diversity

The old varieties are rare in supermarkets, so take the opportunity to grow them in your garden! Also, by cultivating your vegetable garden, you will harvest the right vegetable at the right time, and not all at the same time, a pleasure to rediscover! And why not cultivate original vegetable plants to surprise your friends? Discover our exceptional selection!

6- Stimulate Your Creativity

Gardening is a rewarding personal creation. Acting on its surroundings to beautify it and see the result from day to day and from season to season, provides great satisfaction and stimulates creativity.

7 - For the aesthetic aspect

Greening our cities and cultivating our land means improving our living environment while taking advantage of unused spaces. Terraces, roofs and parking lots are all areas of experimentation for urban vegetable gardens! Also, the presence of greenery in our daily environment considerably improves our well-being! Even in the office, green plants improve our productivity!

8 - Learn from nature

How do our foods grow? Essential for children ... like adults. The garden is a real school. So if you want to learn, you have to practice. You will take the opportunity to teach your children a lot of your knowledge about insects, vegetables and believe me if your child participates in the vegetable garden you will no longer hear "I don't like" at mealtime!

9 - Become aware of ecological issues

Learn to recycle, save water in the garden, grow vegetables and discover that hybrid varieties (non-reproducible) are a great scam that is increasingly fattening large multinationals, learn why agriculture has lost its diversity ... yes, all of this awareness of ecological issues and problems.

10 - It benefits biodiversity

By gardening in harmony with nature and without using pesticides, the positive consequences will be great in relation to biodiversity. Your green corner will be a haven of peace for pollinating insects and butterflies. This is all the more important in urban areas, where green areas are sometimes very little present!

As you can see, there's no lack of reasons for growing your own vegetables, so what do you expect? It's time to start gardening and draft your plan for next season's vegetable garden! If your vegetable patch is already growing your own vegetables, what are the reasons for that? Is it just a matter of culture, enjoyment ... Perhaps just to find out what you've got on your platter?

Vegetables to grow in your home garden

Cultivating the vegetable garden on the balcony or in the home garden is stimulating and fun, and nowadays also trendy. It makes you earn health, joy, and why not, even in your wallet. Even for those who don't have too much space, we have seen that there are various do-it-yourself vertical garden solutions and just use a little trick to transform your terrace into a splendid urban garden. But what to cultivate? Here, in our opinion, the easy vegetables that are easy to grow, even for those who are beginners with gardening techniques.

1) Tomatoes (Lycopersicon esculentum)

Originally from South America, tomato is a creeping plant, and for this reason, it is necessary for most varieties to install support. It is rich in nutrients such as niacin, potassium and phosphorus, antioxidant substances such as lycopene, carotene and anthocyanins, vitamins A, C and E. Thanks to their juicy pulp, tomatoes can add a load of taste and flavor to a variety of dishes, such as salads, pasta and sandwiches.

Choose a place in your garden with good exposure to sunlight after the winter with its frosts and make sure the acidity of the soil is between six and seven pH. (Add lime to increase the pH level, instead add sulfur to decrease.) Get some good compost (or better yet do it yourself) and mix it with the soil. Dig a hole for each seed, separating it from each other about thirty centimeters to allow the plants to expand, cover it, and slightly press the soil. Water with the aid of a spray bottle several times a week.

2) Radishes (Raphanus sativus)

Originating in the Chinese and Japanese areas, it is mainly grown for its roots, the edible portion which can be of different colors (red, white, green, purple), shape and height. Radishes are a great source of potassium, folic acid, magnesium and calcium, and are widely used as a seasoning as well as a basic garnish in salads.

The best time for outdoor sowing is from April to July and, to grow, they need a very sunny soil with a pH of six or seven. They can be planted in both broadcasters and rows. The seeds have to be buried a few centimeters below the surface, being careful to leave ample space between them to allow good plant growth. They do not need abundant but regular watering, for they fear drought. Radish is an annual plant, with a very rapid cycle of production.

3) Zucchini (Cucurbita pepo)

Apparent to a cucumber, this elongated vegetable made its debut in Italy around 1800. It has a low-calorie content with its characteristic green color and is rich in potassium, folic acid and manganese. Zucchini can be boiled, fried, steamed or cooked in the sun as suggested by us. They could be an excellent side dish, a delicious filling or a delicious appetizer.

Sowing will take place between March and May, by placing two or three seeds on each hole. Depending on the variety we'll pick, the holes will be more or less wide. The dimensions for the winter ones will be 50x50x50, while a hole of 30x30x30 will be sufficient for the summer variety. The holes must be lined with compost and spaced at least one meter. The seeds are to be covered by a twenty-centimeter layer of soil. Water generously every day, and in a few weeks, you will see your seedlings sprout.

4) Beetroot (Beta vulgaris)

Beetroot is a biennial cycle plant with a fleshy root which can be boiled or eaten alone or in a salad. Betaine is considered to boost the health of the cardiovascular system as one of the key nutrients in this strong red or purple crop.

The first thing to do is clean and strengthen the seeds by immersing them in the water at room temperature for a day. By removing any stones, we prepare the ground and plant the seeds individually by spacing them apart and watering them at least once a day.

5) Carrots (Daucus carota)

The species is native to temperate regions of Europe and is rich in vitamins A (Betacarotene), B, C, PP, D and E, as well as mineral salts and starches, antioxidants and dietary fibers, of distinctive orange color. Carrots are a delicious and healthy snack, which is an excellent ingredient for cakes to be steamed, baked or boiled.

The sowing can be done according to the varieties from January to October, and it is advisable to do so every 15-25 days in a scalar manner to obtain roots of different sizes. The holes are spaced apart and are to host a few seeds each. The soil must always be well moist, and the quantity of water will decrease as plants mature.

6) Spinach (Spinacia oleracea)

Spinach, originally from south-western Asia, was introduced to Europe about 1000, but only during the nineteenth century, it became increasingly popular as food. This plant's dense green leaves are eaten up, very high in iron and calcium.

Prepare the soil for sowing with compost and bury the seeds a few centimeters deep, holding the right distances to allow the plants to grow properly. Water is ample.

7) Peas (Pisum sativum)

Pea, originally from the Mediterranean and near-eastern area, is an annual herbaceous plant of the Fabaceae family and is a good source of vitamins A, B and C.

Mix the soil with a nutrient-rich compost and consider that abundant watering will be needed to make peas flourish. Spread the seeds a few centimeters apart and plant them to a depth of four-five centimeters.

8) Peppers (Capsicum annuum)

The pepper is an annual Mediterranean herb and a seasonal climate in the warm countries of South America from which it comes. It is rich in vitamins and nutrients such as thiamine, folic acid and manganese, and can be used and seasoned in different ways, both cooked and raw.

Fertilize the soil with both compost and Epsom salts, thereby making it more magnesium-rich to make the peppers grow healthier. They bury the surface seeds since they grow best in warm soils. Water periodically, keeping the soil moist. Otherwise, it can get a bitter taste after you harvest your peppers.

9) Lettuce (Lactuca Sativa)

It is an annual plant with more or less large, ovoid or elongated leaves and it has different shades of color depending on the variety, ranging from green to yellowish to red.

It was considered an aphrodisiac in ancient Egypt. Lettuce is a good source of folic acid and vitamin A. Used as the main ingredient in most salads, and this green leafy vegetable can also be stuffed with different ingredients, of which there are dozens of popular varieties.

Before cultivating the soil, fertilize it with nutrients and work it by removing any stones or debris. Make sure the seeds are planted at a depth of between eight and sixteen centimeters and water every morning.

10) Onion (Allium cepa)

The first signs date back to the Bronze Age. It is a herbaceous biennial plant with a collated root system, rich in fiber, folic acid and vitamin C These bulb vegetables add flavor to a large variety of food items, including sauces, soups, salads and more.

To allow the bulb to grow homogeneously, the soil must be very light, and for this, it must be worked vigorously and free from debris. It is enriched with compost. Plant the seeds a few centimeters deep and well-spaced apart. And this sector is often but gentle and every week provides them with about an inch of water.

CHAPTER NINE
Types of Fertilizer for your garden

You will be faced with the need for fertilizer some time in your gardening, whether you cultivate vegetables or flowers. Nevertheless, many of the commercially available fertilizers are produced from chemical processes that are harmful to the environment. Natural alternatives are available, which will keep your gardens, family and earth safe.

Some of the best things you can do to feed your plants for your garden is not to pick the grass clippings. Let the clippings remain on the grass, instead of using a catcher on your mower. They'll decompose easily and bring essential nutrients back to your lawn. Fast, simple, and free-natural fertilization do not get much better.

Find seaweed, either gathered on its own or bought in the liquid extract from your garden center, for your vegetable and flower beds. This diamond is filled with minerals and trace elements; besides, if worked into the whole soil, its composition tends to help hold the plant's moisture. Most gardeners say this is the only fertilizer you'll ever have to use, and it's completely chemical-free.

When you have access to animal manure, consider using it; it's full of the nitrogen which your plants need. It's better to use rotted down manure, however, because fresh manure will burn the roots of your plants. All kinds of organic manure can be bought, from sheep and cows to the more exotic bat guano. Once it's worked into the soil, it's not nearly as smelly as you might think.

Many natural fertilizers that enjoy large use are blood and bone meal, beer (yep, beer), and coffee grounds.

Nonetheless, make sure that your soil is tested before adding something. You do not have to add something or add just one or two things, such as lime. You can't add anything. More is not better in fertilizer matters, and most plants can do well with a wise eye. You will assist with the soil check and the definition of your local county extension office so that you know exactly what you're dealing with. When you are dealing with your garden, it is always better to be safe than sorry!

Nutrient requirements of garden plants

Plants mainly need macronutrients, i.e., nitrogen, phosphorus and potassium:

- Nitrogen (chemical symbol N). It contributes to the development of foliage and stems or branches. It is an important fertilizer in the spring when the vegetation is recovering. But beware, used in excess, not only pollutes

the water and the soil, but it unbalances the plants, which then produce more leaves at the expense of flowers and fruits. The most nitrogen-intensive plants are grass, grasses, bamboo and leafy vegetables.
- Phosphorus (chemical symbol P). It contributes to the development of the roots, and it strengthens the resistance of plants in the face of diseases. Used in excess, it contributes to the eutrophication of water (that is to say, the proliferation of algae). The most demanding plants in phosphorus are flowering and fruiting species, as well as seed vegetables.
- Potassium (chemical symbol K). It contributes to flowering and fruit development. The most demanding plants in potassium are fruit trees, flowering shrubs, roses, bulbs and root vegetables.

In variable proportions, the fertilizer can only have 1 or 2 elements or blends 3. Numbers showing the exact composition are accompanied by the initials of NPK. The fertilizer containing 16% nitrogen (N), 5% phosphorus (P) and 5% potassium (K) for example NKP 16-5-5 shows.

Plants need secondary nutrients in a lesser extent, such as calcium (C), sulfur (S) and magnesium (Mg), as well as trace elements, such as Iron (Fe), manganese (Mn), copper (Cu), zinc (Zn), silicon (Si), and more. But secondary nutrients are normally present in adequate amounts unless there is a soil deficiency or according to its PH. It is best for your soil to be tested before any fertilizer supply to learn its strengths and imbalances.

The different types of fertilizers

Macronutrients, secondary nutrients, and trace elements come from different sources. Thus nitrogen is present in dried blood, which is an organic fertilizer and in nettle manure, which is considered as an ecological fertilizer. Phosphorus comes from phosphate rock, so it is a mineral fertilizer, but it is also found in bone powder, which is an organic fertilizer. The same is true for potassium. Without forgetting that N, P, and K can also come from the chemical industry... It is, therefore, not by their composition that we can recognize this or that type of fertilizer but rather by their manufacture or their origin.

- Chemical fertilizers: These are synthetic products made from chemical elements.
- L are organic fertilizers: They are of animal origin (Powder bones or fish bones, dried blood, crushed horn, guano) or vegetable (algae, nettle manure or comfrey, ash, the residue of vinasse sugar beet, etc.).
- Mineral fertilizers: They come from natural deposits of inert minerals such as potash or phosphate. But most of the time, they are actually made from chemical elements.

- Ecological or natural fertilizers: These are natural mineral fertilizers, organic fertilizers when they come from natural plant or animal materials. Nettle, comfrey purines are considered ecological fertilizers.
- Green manures: These are fast-growing plants (clover, alfalfa, lupine, horse bean, etc.), which are sown and buried on-site to provide a natural fertilizer rich in organic matter. In the garden, before installing a lawn, it is a good way to fertilize the soil.

CHAPTER TEN
Pests, prevention and treatment

Most Common Pests In Your Garden

Insects are always present in our garden. Many times we think that all can harm our plants, but that is not true. Learn about the most common pest insects in the garden, their characteristics and what you can do to control them.

Aphids

Aphids are a tiny fly, measuring 0.9-3 mm. There are over 4,000 species, but some 250 are considered pests. Its color may be gray, white, red or black, and there are wings in some species. Its mouth apparatus is a sucker, meaning it feeds on the plant's sap. We can find plenty of vegetables, like lettuce, tomato, eggplant, cauliflower, spinach, chili, kale, etc. Aphids transmit diseases, so monitoring our plants is very important. We can find them at the leaves and growth points on the underside.

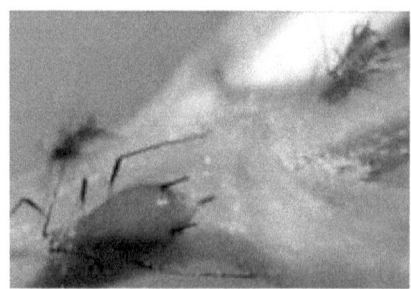

1 Red Aphids

To cool them we can add water on the underside of the plants with biodegradable soap, do it really early in the morning or in the afternoon when the sun does not touch the plants anymore. Some natural enemies of aphids are parasitic wasps (Aphelinus abdominals, Aphidius colemani, Aphidius ervi), Catarina (Coccinellidae), lacewing (Chrysoperla carnea), parasitic fly (Apidoletes sp)

Larvae or caterpillars

There are various forms of larvae in our garden; various sizes and colors. But what exactly is a larva? Larvae are the juvenile stage of some metamorphosis-bearing insects. The larvae which affect our plants come from butterflies or moths of the night.

2 - Larvae or caterpillar

The larvae can be 1-7 cm in size and can have a black, white, gray, brown color. The larvae are insect chewing and can be located on the underside of the leaves, at the point of growth or in the dirt. They attack most plants in our garden, in this botanical family, in particular broccoli, cauliflower, kale and other plants.

To control them, we can use soap and garlic and chili extract with biodegradable water. Apply very early in the morning or evening when the plants no longer receive the rays of the sun. It's a simple method even to extract them by hand. Some natural larvae enemies are lacewing (Chrysoperla carnea) and the Bt (Bacillus thuringiensis) bacteria.

Whitefly

3 - Whitefly

The whitefly is a small (1mm) powdery white insect. This fly feeds on the sap of the plant, reducing its productivity. A side effect of whitefly is disease transmission. We find it on the underside of the leaves of many plants such as; tomatoes, aubergines, pumpkin, cucumber, flowers such as poinsettia and jamaica, among others. Some natural enemies are the Catarina, lacewing, predatory beetles (Orius sp), parasitic wasps (Encarsia sp). We can also apply soapy water or yellow traps.

Leaf miners

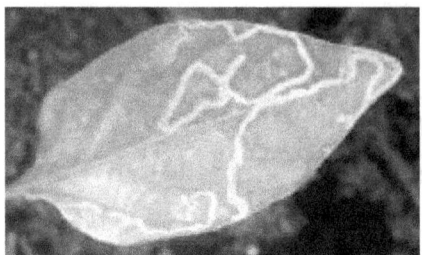

4 - Leaf miners

The leaf miner is a small larva that we can find in the leaves of our plants. They make small galleries or paths between the leaves, taking away space for the plant to carry out its photosynthesis. The most effective control is to locate the larva on the leaf and crush it with our fingers, making sure that you do not hurt the plant.

Chapulines

The chapulines are a common pest that can cause a lot of damage since they eat the leaves and, in some cases, the whole plant. These insects can eat any plant. The grasshoppers can be up to 8cm long. For the control of grasshoppers, we can count on spiders, mantises, Bacillus thuringiensis (Bt, bacteria) and Beauveria bassiana (fungus).

Red spider

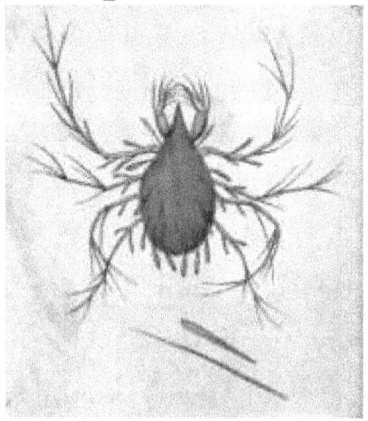

5 - Red Spider[1]

The red spider is a very small insect (0.5mm) that feeds on the sap of plants. Always in a group. These insects form a white spider web on the leaves and stems, thereby protecting themselves from predators. They can attack strawberry, eggplant, squash, tomato, corn, chili, melon, potato, and trees. For its control, an extract of garlic and chili can be applied. If the plant is severely affected, it is best to remove it to avoid spreading to other plants. Good prevention is crop rotation.

Trips

Thrips are small insects that measure between 1-3mm. It is a yellowish-brown or brown color. They feed on the sap of the plant, and they can cause leaf spots and transmit diseases. These insects are attracted to the blue color, and you can put a blue

---

[1] Credit: https://wellcomecollection.org/works/wmcg49n3

container with water and some soap or sticky traps. Thrips have several natural predators, such as some varieties of mites and the Orius bug (Orius sp).

Mealybugs

Mealybugs are small (6mm) black or grayish in color. They feed on the leaves and stems of plants. Very common behavior in mealybugs is that they curl up to protect themselves, forming a small ball. If our soil is well nourished, it will not be a problem for our garden.

Snails and slugs

Snails and slugs are mollusks that live in humid areas and water reservoirs. They feed on all kinds of plants and can end up destroying the entire garden. We can identify the damage by the traces of mucus that they leave behind. We can prevent the arrival of snails by having our plants in elevated places and using aromatic herbs. Remember they are looking for cool and humid places. For its control, we can use coffee beans, beer traps or eggshells.

Nematodes

Nematodes are small plant parasites found in the soil. Its shape is like an earthworm, and they measure between 0.2-1mm depending on the species. These small individuals feed on the roots of the plants, but there are species that are beneficial (they are biological control for some insects). To control the nematodes in the soil, we can plant garlic cloves, and this will serve as a repellent. It is also important to have a crop rotation and fertilize our soil.

You can find many pests in your garden, but controlling them is not that difficult. Remember to check your garden frequently, once or twice a week. Look well under the leaves, and there you can find many pests and other insects.

Vegetable Gardening Problems – Prevention

There are many alternatives to synthetic insecticides to control some unwanted insects that we commonly call as garden pests. It is first important to know which insects are harmful to plants and which are beneficial, the natural allies of the garden. These allies are very important in preventing pests and diseases as they help to protect the plants against some hungry insects that appear more frequently in the spring. There are still other good practices that must be considered in pest prevention!

How to prevent pests in an organic garden

1. Choose the vegetable varieties most resistant to insects and diseases. Whenever possible, we should choose seeds from organic or biodynamic agriculture. In addition, it is preferable to produce seedlings for transplanting.

2. Provide shelter for natural enemies of pests, such as predatory insects (spiders, ladybugs), bats, birds.

3. Improve the soil structure, adding organic compost or making green manure. As a result, healthy soil will allow healthier plants to grow.

4. Grow aromatic and medicinal herbs to bring beneficial insects to the garden. In addition, some have a repellent effect on pests.

5. Try to plant in a small space in order to see if there is damage caused by any present pest. In this way, we understand if there is already a pest installed, and should apply home remedies to control.

6. Cut the first infected plants and remove them from the site. So, by removing the residues from the infected crops, we will help to interrupt the insect's biological cycles.

7. Take into account the practices of favorable intercropping of cultures. Consequently, this practice also helps to benefit from more effective management of soil space and nutrients.

8. Always use natural preventive methods, such as biological control. Furthermore, when they are easily visible, we must collect the pests manually.

9. Avoid monocultures in beds or plots with an area greater than 1 m2. As a result, we promote greater biodiversity, cultivating, for example, some flowering plants such as marigolds, chamomile, capucinhas, among others.

10. Promote crop rotation. Above all, don't grow the same types of vegetables in the same place every year. We can do a 3-year rotation in 3 sites or a 4-year rotation in 4 plots (more advisable).

Treat a garden against pests

Many pests swarm in gardens and attack all plants, whether vegetables, fruit trees or even ornamental plants. Discover how to treat a garden against pests depending on the species you face.

Treat a garden against mealybug

Scale insects generally proliferate on fruit trees from which they suck the sap, causing sores and proliferation of fungi.

To remove them, the use of solutions based on methylated spirits and black soap is necessary. Softer treatment but just as effective: ladybugs, deadly enemies of cochineal.

Fight against aphids

Aphids also suck the sap from plants, slowing their growth. Vectors of viruses and fungi, they readily settle on roses and fruit trees.

Here again, the ladybug can help get rid of the pest, just like nettle manure and repellents (lavender, thyme, mint ...).

Treat plants against snails and slugs

Snails and slugs appreciate the sap of plants and devour their leaves, bulbs, fruits and roots.

The "ramparts" of ash and wood chips installed around the plantations help to slow down these pests. To remove them, there are chemicals based on iron phosphate.

Protect a garden from mites

Some mites (including the red spider) suck the sap from the trees, resulting in desiccation and discoloration of the leaves.

The first bulwark against mites: humidity. Watering the plants well is, therefore, essential. In the case of invasion, there are acaricides, but one can also use the "services" of their predator, Phytoseiulus persimilis.

Treatment against moths

The larvae of the moth (moth) feed on many plants. Leaves, stems, fruits, buds ... are ingested.

Preventive methods to limit egg-laying are essential here: suppress weeds, hoeing, mulching, watering ... If necessary, we will use a phytosanitary product or the Thuringian bacillus (caterpillar killer bacteria).

Treat fruit worm

The codling moth (fruit worm) is a caterpillar that feeds mainly on the flesh of fruits.

To prevent its appearance, there are pheromone traps that limit its fertilization. If necessary, we will spray bacterospeine (natural insecticide) on the affected tree. One can also enshrine spared fruits and destroy those infected.

CONCLUSION

You have many options to escape from the non-productive or poorly grown garden, one of which is how to integrate the advantage of having one or two raised beds in your backyard. A raised bed has advantages over the ordinary bed as you are totally in control of the soil you are using, and you can garden in a more comfortable location. The different soil conditions needed for individual plants can be managed much more effectively and can be varied from bed to bed; a pH soil test kit is a very useful tool for having the right conditions for individual plants.

You will easily get loose, well-drained soil because you do not walk to compact it. Raised garden beds drain much better off surface water, good news for areas with heavy soils and high rainfall than normal garden beds. This will help the plants trap air across the root system, which is a big plus for warm, stable plants.

You should tend your elevated garden bed in a comfortable position to help protect against backaches that can often stop you from trying to supply fresh quality produce for the family. It is also better for people with disabilities or who have to take a seat in the garden. We agree that raised gardens are a great help to any gardener.

There is a range of materials and sizes to choose from when determining whether to create your own garden beds. The availability of space defines the size and number of beds. You can buy kits or build your own from anything that holds dirt, such as wood, plastic, bricks, or rocks very easily. Lumber is the most used and probably the easiest to use.

When planning the raised bed, there are certain things to think about. Decide a comfortable height for you to maintain your plants from any angle without having to walk on the elevated gardens, thus preventing the soil from getting compact. The raised bed should be placed in a position where the plants you want to grow to have a ray of sufficient sunshine, which leaves enough room for wheelbarrows and other tools. In order to address any issues with drainage, elevated gardens should be a minimum of 6 inches in height; it is also prudent to cover the area in order to avoid ruin and soil erosion.

Usually, you just take over the entire dimensions into your garden center when building raised gardens, and they will work out what you need. When you know in advance what plants should be used for your raised garden, it will advise and provide the correct soil mix. We advise you to fill the beds with a half organic matter and a half soil if you raise the beds only up to 15 inches. Know that composting your own reduces your total costs.

Now, if you look at large, three-foot, raised gardens, it is fair that you take a different course of action to produce good results and seek to reduce costs. You may half fill it with rocks or sand to minimize the amount of soil required to fill this wide area, then fill it with a 50-50 mixture of manure or compost and soil. Adjust the pH levels for your plants, and this will give your elevated garden the ultimate conditions for growth.

www.ingramcontent.com/pod-product-compliance
Lightning Source LLC
Chambersburg PA
CBHW070930080526
44589CB00013B/1465